BOOK LOAN

Please RETURN or RENEW it no later
than the last date shown below

sunblue

By
MARGARET AVISON

LANCELOT PRESS

Hantsport, Nova Scotia

ACKNOWLEDGEMENTS

The following poems have previously appeared in these publications:

The Second Mile — *Sounds Carry, Speleologist, Backing into Being, March, Thirst,* and *Embattled Deliverance;*

Toronto Telegram — *Poem on the Astronauts in Apollo XIII's near-disaster, Christmas Approaches,* and *Until-Christmas;*

His magazine — *He couldn't be safe.* This poem was also used by American Inter-Varsity Christian Fellowship on a greeting card;

Exile — *Light (I), Light (II),* and *Midsummer Christmas.*

ISBN 0 - 88999 - 088 - 3

Published 1978

Second printing June 1980

Third printing August 1978

LANCELOT PRESS LIMITED, Hantsport, N.S.

Office and plant situated on Highway #1, one half mile east of Hantsport.

201804

CONTENTS

SKETCH: *Thaws*

The snowflow
nearly-April releases   melting bright.

Then a darkdown
                needles and shells the pools.

Swepth of suncoursing sky
steeps us in
                salmon-stream
                        crop-green
                                rhubarb-coloured shrub-tips:

everything waits for the
lilacs, heaped tumbling — and their warm
licorice perfume.

SKETCH: *Weekend*

On the hall-table a safetypin
under the
small brass fern pot with its
artificial fern.
No dust
but no smell of cooking;
the carpet's corner's curled.

SKETCH: *Overcast Monday*

In this earth-soakt air
we engage with
undeathful technicalities,
hurt that they click.

An oil of gladness, in
the seafloor Light
quickens, secretly.

SKETCH: *A work gang on Sherbourne and Queen, across
from a free hostel for men*

The hostel's winter flies
where morning spills them out
fumble, undisturbed
by street or curb;

paralleled, walled off, by the force
of the through north-south route,
they never meet
the yellow-helmeted men across the street
whose tangling ways, among
dump trucks and crane scoops, put
down, solid and straight,
the new storm sewer conduit.

Both groups go zigzag, veer,
      stand, wait —

but not the same.

SKETCH: *Cement worker on a hot day*

I've passed this yellow hydrant
in sun and sleet, at dusk —
                just a knob
                    shape.

Now, here, this afternoon
suddenly a man
stops work on the new curb in
the oils of sun,

                        and (why of course!)
                        wrenches the hydrant till
                        it yields a gush
                        for him to gulp and wash in.

Yes   yes   a hydrant
was always there but now
it's his, and flows.

SKETCH: *A childhood place*

In the mattressed pasture the
sun's butterfat
    glistens on coarse grass.

    The grassblades scrape.

        ...Seashells of my scattered years
        whiten in the sun...

On the weathered door
wood-hairs leave shadow-lines on the
hot wood.

SKETCH: *CNR London to Toronto (I)*

Grasses bronze and tassel-tawny
knock-kneed trees in little orchard
picnic table frozen in a
backyard tilt beside a thorny
brushheap somebody will burn
with orange flame and lilac smoke
against a cold blue & white sky
some day after the train has long
since fled with us
     and lost
these morning places.

SKETCH: *CNR London to Toronto (II)*

In the Christmas tree and
icing sugar country
they listen under banks
badger foreheads sleek
the sun uncaring, frost
squeaky, bright with
berries: *invisibility.*

SKETCH: *From train window (Leamington to Windsor) in*
March

Miles of beeswax mist,
    a far ravine with fishbone trees,
      one nearer, peacock's quill-fan with
      the violet batik faintly suggested
          by springtime leaflessness;
   rust-spotted   chipped-paint places,
         roadshoulder, gas-pumps,   and a
              flagless metal flagstick;
   somebody's bricks stashed under tarpaulins,
       a wooden bridge in a field and a black
       dog pottily floundering across it:

the pale wintergreen air has
straw stuck to it, and then again becomes
    dimmed in beeswax mist, a
    visual amplitude so still
        that you can hear the hidden culvert gurgle.

The Seven Birds (College Street at Bathurst): SKETCH

Storm-heaped west, wash-soaked with
dayspill.   Light's combers
broken, suds-streaming
            darkwards and stormwards:

        rough roofs
        two-storey store flats
        false gables and futile
    TV aerials   high wire time and
            nobody home yet —
    the stormy sunlit evening children
        whirl with the grit
        and candy-wrapper gusts
    right by the gridwork flow on rails and wheels, under
                            the very shadow of
    heaven and the heavy
    trampling home-bent crowds,
        hoping for supper.

Seven birds toss
skyward and glide
and ruffle down:

    birds on the TV wires
    eye-mirroring the light of the
        wild west.

The floods of blackness
swirl (bells and pomegranate pompoms) in.

SKETCH: *End of a day: OR, I as a blurry*

I as a blurry groundhog bundling home
find autumn storeyed:

       underfoot is leafstain and gleam of wet;
       at the curb, crisp weed
       thistled and russeted;
       then there's the streetlight level;
       then window loftlights, yellower;
       above these, barely, tiers
       of gloaming branches,
       a sheet of paraffin-pale wind,
       then torn cloud-thatch and
       the disappearing clear.

Indoors promises
such creatureliness as disinhabits
a cold layered beauty
flowing out there.

Grass Roots

There is a grass-roots level:
small ears and weed-stems;
necklacing ant-feet; robins' toe-pronging and beak-thrust;
raindrops spotting in,   or
cratered, sluicing, and wrenching
grass flat, gouging
earth, to enrich.

Summer is so.

Winters, that level
is ore, deep under snow.

Stone's Secret

Otter-smooth boulder
lies under rolling
black river-water
stilled among frozen
hills and the still unbreathed
blizzards aloft;
silently, icily, is probed
stone's secret.

Out there — past trace
of eyes, past these
and those memorial skies
dotting back signals from
men's made mathematics (we
delineators of curves and time who are
                    subject to these) —
out there, inaccessible
to grammar's language the
stones curve vastnesses,
cold or candescent
in the perceived
processional of space.

                    The stones out there in the
                    violet-black are part of a
                    slow-motion fountain? or of a
                    fireworks pin-wheel?
                    i.e. breathed in and out
                    as in cosmic lungs? or
                    one-way as an eye looking?
What mathematicians must,
also the pert,
they will
as the dark river runs.

Word has arrived that
peace will brim up, will come

"like a river and the
glory...like a flowing stream."
So.
Some of all people will
wondering wait
until this very stone
utters.

Hid Life

Red apples hang frozen
in a stick-dry, snow-dusty
network of branches,
against lamb's wool and pastelblue of sky,
a crooked woodenness, a wizzening red.

Are these iron stems? or is
this tree in a lee out of the
clattering winds?

Heavily in my heart
the frost-bruised fruit, the sombre tree,
this unvisited room off winter's endless corridors
weigh down.

       But
even this fruit's flesh
will sodden down at last.

Botanist, does the seed
so long up held
still somehow inform
petal and apple-spring-perfume
for sure, from so far?

Is the weight only
a waiting?

Released Flow

In the sunward sugarbush
runnels shine and down-rush
through burning snow and thicket-slope.
The spiced air is ocean-deep.

Melting ridge and rivermouth
shape the waters in the earth
and the motions of the light
close the flow as watertight.

> "In and out the windows"
> squirrels flip and play
> through sunsplash and high and low
> in winter's gallery.

The extraordinary beyond the hill
breathes   and is   imperturbable.
Near the gashed bough the hornets fur
in paperpalace-keep and -choir.

Across snowmush and sunstriped maples
honeyed woodsmoke curls and scrolls.
Sunblue and bud and shoot wait to unlatch
all lookings-forth, at the implicit touch.

March Morning

The diamond-ice-air is ribbon-laced
with brightness.   Peaking wafering snowbanks are
sun-buttery, stroked by the
rosey fingertips of young
tree shadows
as if for music;
and all the eyes of God glow, listening.

My heart branches,
swells into bud and spray:
heart break.

The neighbour's kid
lets fall his mitts
shrugs jacket loose
and wondering   looks   breathing the
crocus-fresh   breadwarm
Being —
easy as breathing.

March

A Caribbean airflow
shampoos the brook.
The deepsea deepwarm look of
sky wakes green below
amid the rinds of snow.

Though all seems melt and rush,
earth-loaf, sky-wine,
swept to bright new horizons
with hill-runnel, and gash,
all soaked in sunwash,

far north, the ice
unclenches, booms
the chunks and floes, and river brims
vanish under cold fleece:
the floods are loose!

Then sullen torn
old skies through tattery trees
clack, freezing
stiffens loam; the worn
earth's spillways then relearn
                    how soaring bliss
                    and sudden-rigoring frost
                    release
                    without all lost.

Highway in April

Last year's grass-mat
thickens thatchily
over the inward-
stirring valley.

The cars roll on, as does
the striped, rampstripping, wireless
highway, sloped to a rain-sheen
illusion.

Under the car-roofs faces
blur by each other,
all the dark inwardnesses
softened in this weather.
(There is a whole underground sea
under the prairies.)

Sheer up, the sun
stands whole: the warmth
soaks in, till all
alive come forth.

Let Be

Behind the rainmurk
is, I persuade myself,
a mountain shouldering
near enough   one might mark
— but for the rain — the treeline
from the implausible plateau of this
Parisgreen cow pasture
watered by a
meander (old river now a
ditch brimming over into
frog-marsh), this side of
the massive roots
of light,   of rain,   of
mountain-range.

Let there be
splashings, shouts,
dogs gnawing, oarlocks,
or people's random opinions
on a battery radio,
or the precise   other   inevitable
alternative — as will be plain —
to give ballast in daylight
to the unseen mountain's
no-sounding soundness.

Water and Worship: an open-air service on the Gatineau River

On the pathway mica glints.
Sun from the ripple-faceted water
shines, angled, to gray cliffs and the blue sky:
      from up here the boat-braided river is
      wind-riffled, fishes' meadows.
                  But at
            eye-level, on the dock, the water looks deep,
                    cold, black, cedar-sharp.
            The water is self-gulping under
            clefts and pier posts.

We listen.
your all-creating stillness, shining Lord,
trembles on our unknowing
               yearning
                       yielding lives:
      currents within us course
      as from released snow, rock-
      sluiced, slow welling from
               unexpected hidden springs,
    waters still acid,
    metallic with old wrecks —
            but Love draws near,
            cut-glass glory, shattering everything
                          else in
            the one hope known:

            (how are You so
            at home with what we know?)

The waters lap.
Rocks contain and wait
in the strong sun.

          "Joyful, joyful, we adore Thee...."

Sounds Carry

Nimbus of summer
undefines place and
time imitates an immemorial dawn
                    — dogs at the white gates....
Breathing is palpable, and
breathes response to amplitude
and hidden tendril,
yearning for large and little;
and calm birds pick about their toes
or settle, riffling, down.

Misty summer
sidetracks years
to disused loading sheds sweet with the
sun on worn boards ... flies
and bird cheepings ...
a clarity beyond the mist
within the nimbus of this summer's now.

Thirst

In the steeped evening
deer stand, not yet
drinking
beyond the rim of here;

and crystal blur
clears to the jet
stream, pure, onflowing:
a not yet known —

beyond the grasses where the deer

stand, deep in evening
still.

"While as yet no leaves may fall"
                                    (William Barnes)

I came on a spare corner in time,
an empty angle, in a broken light;
the sound of voices from committee-rooms
came distantly (like the irrelevant
clatter at noon in hospital hallways
to the patient immured in the last
lucid wash of light).   From somewhere near
pigeons were burbling, and motors sighed,
but only soughed the surface.

                        The back stairs
in old farmhouses create space like this.

In the wayside chapel a stiff bunch
of old bouquet rustles to the wind.

The evening meadows wait   under the willow trees.

Morning Bus

A bird is flattened on the road's shoulder.
The feathers fibrillate
as the slowed bus sighs.

Through the bus's gills
the nearing lake air
breathes in.   We breathe:

something is nonetheless, foul —
fish in the stew of time
flaked, on green sand? the
bulky buildings sweating rancid stove oil?

The feathers flutter
on unflyable wings
wadded in morning-drying clay.

We breathe.
We jolt.   This slump of letting be
refuses fusion; it is a
non-homogeneity that goes on.

For each, enough
is destination.

A Lament

A gizzard and some ruby inner parts
glisten here on the path where wind has parted
the fall field's silken ashblonde.

I fumble in our fault
("earth felt the wound," said Milton).
Cobwebs of hair glued
to cheekbone, among
gnat eddies and silences,
I clamber on through papery leaves and slick
leathering leaves between
the stifling meadows.

Eyeblink past blue, the far
suns herd their flocks.

Crumbling comes,
voracious, mild as loam —
but not restoring. Death has us glassed in
for all the fine airflow and the
auburn and wickerwork beauty of this valley.

Somewhere a hawk swings, stronger,
or a weasel's eyes brighten.

The viscera still shine
with sun, by weed and silver riverflow.

The Evader's Meditation

"I want to be whole
never mind what it costs —
anaesthesia, pill
skin-graft, cast — ...."

                    Oh, it cost.
                    The whole
                    heart was glutted
                    with us, turned inside out...

"Well, even that, if
therapies leave
nothing else I can try.
I want to be whole and okay before I die."

                    In what glass
                    do you look to assess
                    this physique of yours?
                    the Book?   or the people-pleaser's?

"What I expected was clearer
before you mentioned the mirror....
What time can I come back?
Next week?"

On?

There is a direction? And it's
  on?
        Toughly and cheerily
        the pathfinders encourage
        at the last stepping-stone
                  ("There
                    we are!")
If it is on, then
    where we know, or
    where we're going to,
        is all one?

    ....
Yoo hoo.
Dark.   A whiplash branch — I'm holding it — are you
                              there?
    Whose
    breathing?
    (No one's?)
No no no. No
more, I don't like being left
        alone like this.

On is the planet's —
earth-rush, girth-swivel, candlepower to the nth —
    not mine. I
    lie brambled biting on a
              root.
    Wait!   Wait for whoever (me?)
      is out here in this
      thickety wild place!

O day breaking — away down engraved and embossed on the
      sheen of water:
                On would've been OVER I tell you. I
                hung onto this wind-ragged tag of a
                bush, not-going in time -- it's the
                sheer edge almost.   I hung
"On?"
      Yes.

A Work-Up

THE ANGEL OBSERVES

> lips, as if stone-carved,
> cold, the grit lying unfanned and
> sand-dry — an engine-hood of a
> cathedral, cabaret spot-lights —
> moving to speak....

THE ANGEL ENTERS.

> (Mildly):
> > "What *are* you about?
> > You're itting yourself."

(The wind suspires.)

> The astonied eyelids
> fail even to blink.

THE ANGEL BEGINS TO LEAVE:

> "Wind and light want to be bare
> to your unringing ear,
> beloved.   Oh, beware!"

Contemplatives: OR, Internal Combustion

Around 4 a.m.
the hermits come
and gun a jalopy
apiece down the empty
unseen car-track

past the sealed air-controlled
night-hollowed office blocks
and jumbled dormitory blocks
with windows cranked half open
or windows hoisted up
and blinds tap tapping.

Deadly down these
roofless tunnels the hermits
clatter and boom,
spanging bullets of sound
around and further away
and away.

By busying 6 a.m.
out along ditch canals
beyond the horsefarms and the mushroom sheds
under the chassis they sleep
or over the wheel
waiting out daylight-solitude,
getting set to rev up,
again.

Technology is Spreading.

Two men hatless plodding
behind, in the rain,
one to the other confiding,
set this strategem:

> "When using a
> computer it is always desirable
> to stick to one language."

"These words," said memory,
"have come unsung —
but note (in case of 'always'
or too many a sticky tongue)."

And yet, one "stuck" to
who could "desire"?
Just today's luck to
so catch unfire.

Two men, one fair-haired
one nearly bald
passed unimpaired had
while the rain squalled.

Strong Yellow, for Reading Aloud:
                    written for and read to English 385's
                    class when asked to comment on my
                    poem "The Apex Animal", etc.

A painted horse,
a horse-sized clay horse, really,
like blue riverclay, painted,
with real mural eyes — or a
Clydesdale with his cuff-tufts
barbered — the mane
marcelled like a conch and cropped and plastered down like a
merry-go-round pony's
without the varnish —
all kinds confounding,
yet a powerful presence
on the rainy Sunday diningroom wall,
framed by a shallow niche ...

Q: "Miss Avison could you
        relate that to the 'head of a horse'?"

No. No. That one
was strong yellow — almost tangerine, with
white hairs, the eyes
whited too as if
pulled back by the hair
so the eyeballs would water with wind in them,
one you'd call Whitey, maybe,
though he was not, I say,
white ...

Q: "Auburn?"

It was not a horse-shaped horse,
or sized. It loomed. Only the
narrow forehead part, the
eyes starting   loose and appled,
and shoulder-streaming part....
Colour? a stain on the
soiled snow-mattress-colour of

40

the office-day noon-hour mezzanine
        that is the sky downtown.

Q: "The Head of the Horse
      'sees', you say in that poem.
      Was that your vision of
      God, at that period
      in your development?"

Who I was then we
both approach timorously —
or I do, believe me!
But I think, reading the lines,
the person looking *up* like that
was all squeezed solid, only a crowd-pressed
mass of herself at shoulder-
level, as it were, or at least
nine to noon, and the p.m. still to come
day *in* day *out*   as the saying goes
which pretty well covers everything
or seems to, in *and* out then,
        when it's like that: no heart, no surprises, no
people-scope, no utterances,
no strangeness, no nougat of delight
           to touch, and worse,
no secret cherished in the
midriff then.
Whom you look up from that to
is Possibility not
God.
     I'd think ...

Q: "Strong yellow."

Yes!   Not the clay-blue
with rump and hoof and all and almost
eyelashes, the pupil
fixed on you, on that wall of
fake hunt, fake aristocracy
in this fake Sunday
diningroom I was telling
about....

Condeminstrel copia
the archway read.
Not to go in
would unframe my head.

Inside the court
a fountain dribbled
so I stayed on and
hourly sibylled.

Nobody expected
commerce or coin
each one teaching
his own-bound voisin.

One wore a stilts,
one a daubed top-hat.
Well, among us
we were satisfat.

The chestnut leaves
rotted us under
and you'll find that archway
now a choke of cumber.

Sestina (1964)

Eyes keen, because you licked sticky wood-honey,
Jonathan?   You shrug at a rumoured fast
for scared unequipped men.   They quail to see
these fierce Philistines milling around in their blood,
earth heaving underfoot, friends' faces hostile
enough to kill first, under the dire bright arc.

From the felt virtue of the holy ark
how should Saul, king of the tribes, extract the honey?
A father, he stands tall, hasty not hostile.
The household that holds Jonathan fast
outshines royalty's luminary, through blood,
as this wild breakfast gives the son to see.

In the printed Word, I, astigmatic, see
your name, in the sacred calorescence an arc-
lamp bright through my carbon generation's blood.
The enemy braces our leaf-stuck stoney honey-
combing metropolis.   Our young heroes are fast
with a buck.   And the holy licks at us all as if hostile.

Is it the host on earth now that makes us all hostile?
Our day too soars, a cliff where the prince could see
the follower doggedly climbing, breathing fast.
Tales puddle down to magic, or moviehouse arc-
hitecture in celluloid: 'Jonathan has a honey,
his at the cliff-top, coy till he risks his blood!'

Samuel's grief was harsh, foreboding the blood.
The priest is no popular leader.   Don't tell us the hostile
megatons hide under that affluent honey
of words.   We cover our ears.   We do not see
the mercy in the flood story about the ark
for paired progenitors, though it still hold fast.

The young, sensing aliens all sides these days, fast,
too angry to earn or eat, afraid of blood.
A million candle-per-sq.-inch project the arc

down, on the graph. Fortune and time are hostile.
Most are forlorn. Self-exiled a few see
their land out with the locusts and wild honey.

Who dares any longer break fast, dares be not hostile?
The Son's blood clears a dawning arc — oh see
Him with aghast disciples, sharing the fish, the honey.

Embezzler (I): His Act (Luke 16)

The "unjust steward"
        called to account
invoked the principle of quid-pro-quo:
a little kindness, scattered in a
mesh of diminished debts and muted
        obligations made a
        stunt-man's safety net.
At least the others' debts didn't seem appalling
        when his own were plain past hope of more
                                                stonewalling.

Anyway, who could honourably venture
fairness to Mammon's lord, being his creature?
His shrewdness actually tickled the manager
and — "good PR" — made the firm feel
taking the loss still worked a general benefit.

The storyteller knew
their world: the rich man and the steward,
customers, sheds, primary industries, the
sea and airways, the
delicate networks of blood, breath's come and
go, the dark lord and the quick
wit too. He knew about people's
nimbleness when caught.

He dares to let the
wisdom of the world
commend that steward's feathering of his nest:
so a closed world of rascals
closes in lord and vassals
with what they choose.

Embezzler (II): A Classic Case?

The truth is, all we "have"
is not owned.   How we appropriate
                this goody and that, and pad
                the books, quick to do favours
                from somebody else's coffers!

        O yes   our accounts look good.

                We almost thought that we
                had made it, had it made.

When we're called to account
there's — fleetingly — relief:
we really cannot ever make it good.
But quick, before we're out
on the street,
fiddle those final ledger entries
so made friends may provide from well-stocked pantries.

Embezzler (III): "...wiser than the children of light"?

Taught and furnished richly   but in debt
by not living it out
we can be stiff when caught

and duck the blame
and in haste in another's name
on lesser small-claims culprits lower the boom.

Wasting goods in trust
can go so far it cuts
a man completely off his storehouse access.

Yet who could feed
that steward, fired,
except the backdoor beneficiaries of the same affluent lord?

Embezzler (IV): The Wastrel Begins to Hope.

But who's really in charge?

The friends he eased
met his necessities
despite his years of waste.

> Brimming hours of days
>   and fruit of the sun
> are trusts; also the powers
> in one physique burning, and around him
> in others' energies.   All fit
> into a brimming life-ful-ness, an
> everywhere poise of parts in their best places.

To never waste minutes, muscle,
money,
would be to not fail.

Yet, failing, this man still
was not quite wasteful
      employing all he had
for those who would be able to provide:
the story does not call *him* "good"!

> There has been One who proved trust-
> worthy.   He does not waste
> a word.   Stripped bare to give, He then
> entrusts, awarded all as His possession.

For the Murderous: The Beginning of Time

Cain brought grain on his forearm
                    and a branch with grapes
         to the plain earth
         under the wide sky:
vaguely he offered   to the far-borne light
what the slow days had sweetened.

Abel killed, from his flock.
On the fire he made sacrifice.
Fat-brisk rose smoke and sparks,
and blood darkened the stone place.

              That this was "better" than that
              kindled in Cain a murderer's heart —
              he was watched over, after; but he kept apart.

In time the paschal lamb
before the slaying did
what has made new the wine
and broken bread.

All Out; OR, *Oblation* (as defined in 2 Sam. 23, 13-17
& 1 Chron. 11, 17-19)

Where sandstorms blow
and sun blackens and withers, licks up
into empty bright glare
any straggler
        who is exposed
                being still alive,
there:
    clean   cold   water
      throat-laving
      living
        water.

    Look! — a little group of men:
    sun flashes
    on the water poured from leather pouch
    into a bowl, shining,
      now uplifted.
God.
God.
    Saltwater has etched
    their cheeks, their mouthcorners.

WHAT ARE THEY DOING?
They are crazy. They are
      pouring it
        out.
Sand coats the precious drops and darkens with the life-stain.
                                     Earth's
    slow and unspasmodic swallowing is slowly, slowly
                          accomplished.
No. I do not understand,

yet with the centuries still gaze at them
    to learn to expect to
    pour it out

    into desert — to find out what it is.

Dryness and Scorch of Ahab's Evil Rule:
                              Elijah said, this way
                              comes no refreshing,
                              only famine, drought.
                                      (I Kings 17)

Elijah's raven was a bird
of prey, a scavenger.
And yet he was — Elijah heard
it right — God's messenger.

His wafer from no holy fire:
"this grisly flesh — or die".
Cherith Brook alone was pure
and Cherith too went dry.

Elijah swallowed what the bird
of doom there dangled down
until the desert.   Then the word
came, and he could go on.

A widow had not needed ravens.
Now her one son lay starving.
Elijah begged.   "Well, all I have is
gone, if I risk serving"....

She did.   The boy lived on;
the prophet still endures:
the unfailing meal and oil a sign
to last through centuries.

It consecrates a time
of bony men and doom
lit towards the bread and drink of Him
whose is the final kingdom.

He Couldn't be Safe (Isaiah 53:5)

He chose a street
where he wouldn't be safe
and nobody there would save him.

He went to the parties
that were not safe
not saying who, but they knew him.

He went down the road
to the Place of the Skull.
The soldier was there, and the criminal,
and the ones who thought if he didn't have pull
they wouldn't be safe to know him.

He couldn't be safe
and come where we
go, and hide,
and storm, and agree
on everything else if only he
wouldn't show up our artful way
with the light of his simplicity.

No.   He couldn't be safe and be
our Saviour.

To Emmaus

"Are you the only stranger in Jerusalem
who has not heard?"
The Risen One wandered their road with them.
Their beclouding had not cleared
and did not lift even from
His word.
He simply came when asked at evening
and broke bread there, a third, with them.
And abruptly they were assured,
beyond all that seeing had suffered
joyful.   They hurried
to those who had not heard.

"The Lord is risen indeed,"
the welcomers cried.

As a Comment on Romans 1:10 —
> "I saw the Lord always before me/
> Therefore my heart was glad and
> my tongue rejoices."

Paul petitioned to go
to Rome "by any means"
and was led by the centurion
to the Emperor's death-row.

Yet he urged it.   He was
glad these new Romans existed.
His wisdom was enlisted as
their ally, to find them his.

It did not save his neck
or probably theirs:
he knew beforehand that when light appears
it must night split   and earth quake.

The Circuit (Phil. 2, 5-11)

The circuit of the Son
in glory falling
not short
and without any clutching after
His Being-in-Light,
but stripping, putting on
the altar-animal form
and livery of Man
       to serve men under orders
       to, into, death,
       trusting the silent Glory
       (though at that instant out of touch) —
            flesh marred, heart
            deliberately benighted
            till the spilt Blood on the criminals' hill
            split earth and Temple veil
            (then all was silent,
            cloth-cased and closed in a stone hole) —
      to prise, till touching with unflickering Breath
He prises even us free:

this circuit celebrates the Father of Lights
who glorifies this Son and all that He
in glory sows
of Light.

The Bible to be Believed

The word read by the living Word
sculptured its shaper's form.
What happens, means.   The meanings are not blurred
by Flood — or fiery atom.

>He reads: a Jewish-Egyptian
>firstborn, not three years old;
>a coal-seared poet-statesman;
>an anointed twelve-year-old.

The Word dwells on this word
honing His heart's sword,
ready at knife-edge to declare
holiness, and come clear.

>Ancient names, eon-brittled eyes,
>within the word, open on mysteries:
>the estranged murderer, exiled, hears at last
>his kinsman's voice;
>the child, confidingly questioning, so close
>to the awful ritual knife,
>is stilled by another, looking to His Father —
>the saving one, not safe.

The Word alive cherishes all:
doves, lambs — or whale —
beyond old rites or emblem burial.
Grapes, bread, and fragrant oil:
all that means, is real
now, only as One wills.

>Yes, he was tempted to wash out
>in covenanting song
>the brand on the dry bone;
>he heard the tempter quote
>the texts he meant and went embodying.

The Word was moved
too vitally to be entombed
in time.   He has hewn out
of it one crevice-gate.

His final silencing endured
has sealed the living word:
now therefore He is voiceful, to be heard,
free, and of all opening-out the Lord.

Listening

Because I know
the voice of the Word
is to be heard
I know I do not know
even my own cast burden,
or oh, the costly load
of knowing undisturbed.
There is a sword
enters with hearing. Lord
who chose being born to die
and died to bring alive
and live to judge
though all in mercy, hear
the word You utter
in me, because I know
the voice.

Light (I)

The stuff of flesh and bone
is given, *datum*. Down
the stick-men, plastiscene-
people, clay-lump children, are strewn,
each casting shadow in the eye of day.

Then — listen! — I see
breath of delighting rise from
those stones the sun touches
and hear a snarl of breath
as a mouth sucks air. And with
shivery sighings — see: they stir
and turn and move, and power
to build, to undermine, is theirs,
is ours.

The stuff, the breath, the power to move even thumbs
and with them, things: *data*. What is
the harpsweep on the heart for?
What does the constructed power
of speculation reach for?
Each of us casts a shadow in the bewildering day,
                              an own-shaped shadow only.

The light has looked on Light.

He from elsewhere
speaks; he breathes impasse-
crumpled hope even
in us:
that near.

Light (II)

That picture, taken from the
wing window, shows a shadow.

High up, between
the last clouds and the airless
light/dark, any shadow is
— apart from facing sunlessness —
self, upon
self.

Nights have flowed;
tree shadows gather; the sundial
of a horizoning hill in Lethbridge measures the
long grassy afternoon.

Still, freed from swallowing downtown blocks of shadow,
I note self-shadow on
        stone, cement, brick,
relieved; and look to the sunblue.

So, now.

Light (III)

Flying Air Canada over
the foxed spread snowy land,
we look where light is shed
from lucid sky on
waters that mirror light.

The magical reflectors there belie
factory   and fall-out   and run-off effluvia.

Where is the purity then,
except from so
feebly far aloft?
Is it a longing, but to be brought to earth,
an earth so poisoned and yet precious to us?

The source of light is high
above the plane.   The window-passengers
eye those remote bright waters.

Interpreters and spoilers since the four
rivers flowed out of Eden,
men have nonetheless
learned that the Pure can bless
on earth *and* from on high
ineradicably.

From a Public Library Window

The uncoiling, jointed, glass-and-duragloss-
plated, flowing
serpent of traffic will
be stilled.

The seemingly stilled, upthrust
office and apartment towers
and smokestacks
will with the slow
of brickdust-Nineveh's flow,
(and even the basking hills)
sift down and be all through.

The tissue moon
still floating in skylake
and the sunflooding sunfire point —
        swivel of food and drink and sense —
from before Adam, wait
for the once opening of
the Golden Gate.

Only the Unchanging One
is, inexhaustibly, un-done.

The Effortless Point

Three long-distance-runners
out for buoyancy
pad by me, leaving the weed tassles a-waggle
and are past the sumach clump and
fleet,   into brightness flowing,
they bear along
                          lungs
                                    all rinsed with morning.

For Richard Rolle, swift in the strength of stillness,
flowed light,   and the   out there   flooded
his pulses
leaping these six centuries —
love breathes him so alive.

Moving into sky
or stilled under it
we are in the becoming
moved: let wisdom learn
unnoticing in this.

Oughtiness Ousted

God (being good) has let me know
no good apart from Him.
He, knowing me, yet promised too
all good in His good time.

This light, shone in, wakened a hope
that lives in here-&-now —
strongly the wind in push and sweep
made fresh for all-things-new.

But o, how very soon a gloat
gulped joy: the kernel (whole)
I chaffed to merely *act* and *ought* —
"rightness" uncordial.

But Goodness broke in, as the sea
satins in shoreward sun
washing the clutter wide away:
all my inventeds gone.

Hope

It was a clear bright world
from a shining source.
           Along the way it has been spoiled,
               gross-warted by the cheap and coarse,
                    inwardly, worse.

     I'd thunderbolt it down
     to shred in withering smoke
     if that way everything could drown
        in all I've found of dark --
     then to-be-born ones in the gold of dawn
     need never even look.

The shining one looked, and said "we",
owning one source with us.
That chokes the heart unbearably;
here, where we grope and fuss,
dully we hear, and dully wonder why
we did Him in for this.

"Why you did? No. I chose to come
and knew the way was through
your flesh and blood and doom
of death. I, judge and lover, knew."

            A death You *chose?*

"First. Yes."

     Somehow a clear bright world
     wakens at the voice.
     The glory has not filled
     His long appointed place
     but shall, because
     He knows.

Contest

Having in Adam chosen to know
we are sorely honoured in
choosing to know, I know.

We do know what we do.
The second Adam chose to know but
to do otherwise, thus condemning
all but the goodness He
thus declares knowable.

Grimly we concede it, who
would rather do and know,
until as we are known we know.

Into the Vineyard: a Vision

Among the quickening thud of wings,
head borne steadily on past the chokecherries' branches —
ears and nape of neck as formal as
Indian pipestem, or sea-wake of
fresh-turned loam, or wings,
all alike breathed by purposes of wholeness —
he goes, straight as a sunshaft, not
ducking from the angel. He
simply walks on.

The sun burns down on all
who linger and who go.

On Goodbye

The radiant distance, not transparent, remarks
calm trees in evening water,
or remote childhood fields, window-seats, quilts,
on the blank hourlessness the old
stare at and so bless;
this distance seals
both parties to outwardness; it is
itself the poignancy it would leave
to that failed place
where no one is.

Distance, through this time I listen to
you, learning not-being, looking through for
an analogous point in vacancy,
with walls of you and me,
as boundaries, set, that that which is not may be.

Intercession

To leave it in God's keeping
is not to turn aside
from the caring or coping
and not saying it's all right.

Is it to discover
when heart and head
are prayer-held, that the members
are to-be-healed?

He knows His body
here   must   be
caught up in and ready
for long-suffering too.

The old saint, because of her
long hours not spent afield
therefore with searching force
waits it out, for us:
wounded, and healed.

As Though

One looks about at the green-hung room of this earth
as though as seed in the soil
still, and about to split
rotting with reaches towards the
inconceivable elsewhere,

knowing no purposing, only
a kind of atavistic feelers-out,
as a comber shells,
arched, day after day, to
shatter waveness.

Nevertheless
becomings are then in now;
unbearable unless
suffered:

hope stirs,
not surges.

Backing into Being

Feathers skinned off
but pinions ribpressed in,
I, squeezed in muffling
dark, go narrowing

knowing a point of light.
The day withdrawn-from here
a funereal ointment
seals off anywhere.

(Dark — With day still in sight?
The hole is from a place:
once as a child I foot-
groped back through a crevice

out onto a sheer cliff;
the sweating fingers slipped;
falling towards rock and surf
my I unslept

memorably.)   Let go
till forced I may not.   Crawl
back to false everyday
is inadmissible.

(That bird — whom I would
love as my neighbour — comes
from the place the tensile cat
twitches, and will pounce?)

I shrink back into dark
towards a threshold of fear,
beak gaping and quills barked
all for hope's lively danger.

The place remembered, and the here distress
still pinpoint for us final skyfulness.

Scar-face

Scarred — beyond what plastic surgery
could do, or where
no surgeon was when blasted
in the wilds or
               on a sideroad —

he prows his life through
the street's flow and wash
of others' looks.

His face is a good
face, looking-out-from.

City Park in July

Walking on thistling grass
in sandals   stepping in the crisp
drought-barnacled grass-crust,
I see a city gardener smoke
through weed-crumbs with his mower.   But
the park pine is still glossy:
its roots stab down, and deep
in, find the winter run-off still.
                    I swallow
depth.   My thirst would fill
dark reservoirs against a
dessicating brightness.

Hope rises very deep.

The Engineer and the Asparagus

Asparagus, once established, bustles
it grows so vehemently,
cone by cone nosing out towards
those (unseen) garbled acres and the sun's
tusks of flaming.

A person — as the dentist meticulously,
            silverly, nicks him out, under
            fluorescence, in a dead air, with the gutters
            tinily gurgling —

a person
compacts his growth, shells over
sore decay spots, and retracts,
            coil upon twanging coil.

Put down the dental floss, the number ten iron,
the gear knob, the wire-clippers, the periscope and fins.
Just put down, for a minute, the obsolete
    stencil-stylus, the ink-pad-stamp, the farmyard
                            gaspump feed-line.

Down tools.   And in
abashed intervals
let us abound
asparagus-like
(straight up through the driveway concrete!)

Neighbours?

At the carstop
in the tarpots' fume
weltered, you walked
past, stranger, like a found
manganese nodule — concentrate
of mortal meaning on the
seafloor of the city's
daytime din.
The streetcar jolted on.

"What speaks?"   The stranger's
face and walk compel
awareness still.

To contemplate is an
indulgence, distancing
a self, an object.
To mine the meaning of
a found identity
will be given only to
recovered innocence.

"Then contain,
content to wait till Then."

To not know when it is the worst is worst

Berries in brambles, loose, or pressed
hammocky by feeding bears:
fresh-water springs, resins, some roots:
fish baked in coals of smarting-sweet shore fires:

    w e   c a n   r e m e m b e r

        though habit-tranced we steer
        the jumbled shopping-cart through supermarket
                                  aisles.

  W e   k n o w   o f   w o r s e. But

     I'd rather outstare
     thirstlessness, where the sub-Sahara shrivels
     and grasslands sift under the glaring skies,
        than have had doctrine I could leave

        as the storybook-picture cook at last abandons
        recipes,   bowls,   and blades
             stove,   spatulas,
        in a foodless,
             garbageless,
                  always sunny and clean

        forever meaningless kitchen.

Where sunlight quietly delights
in wild fruits and clear water —
or where the dry wind serves
as only scavenger:

in both alike, food is
untheoretical.
Known. Or unknown.

Emmanuel

"With us" in this pain
though His is the morning
of all promise, the morning
of only hope,

to be done with it all, there,
now, and choose nonetheless
this place:

in that   in today   in pain
He makes Love plain.

Needy

A) In part, who isn't
          miserly with his need —
          or needled by it —
          or debonair
          as though it were not there —
          or, at best, genuinely free
                to need yet never be
                needy?

B) "The poor are always being
        inspected: by the
                Fire Department, for litter, oily rags, those
                lamp-cords from the washing-machine to
                the hall ceiling socket, etc.;
                      by the
                'worker' with new forms
                to be written on;
                      by the
                mission visitor 'to invite
                you to the children's pageant';
        somebody even inspects
        to check on whether it's true you keep chickens and goats!"

C) Home after a day of calls
        she absent-mindedly pulls
        the curtains first
        and then acknowledges a thirst:
        everything has run out
        again tonight.

We the Poor who are Always with us

The cumbering hungry
and the uncaring ill
become too many
try as we will.

Try on and on, still?
In fury, fly
out, smash shards? (And quail
at tomorrow's new supply,
and fail anew to find and smash the why?)

It is not hopeless.
One can crawling move
too there, still free to love
past use, where none survive.

And there is reason in
the hope that then can shine
when other hope is none.

Ps. 80:1 — "Thou that dwellest between the cherubim, shine forth!"

In autumn dark comes early,
the wind goes to the bone,
the crowds are very busy
and a person feels alone.

You know, Lord, You know us
out in the dark and cold —
and never planned to leave us out
although shut out of old.

The windows of the glory
were open, and You knew
Your power was for outpouring
in time   to make this new.

We didn't know You, Jesus.
You came out in the night
and poked around the side streets
to bring us to Your light.

We waited where the wind blew
and knifed You in the rain.
Yet You still know who's scared and cold
and doesn't dare complain.

Some You have given food and warmth
now can go back out to
be with You in the darkness,
vagrants, focused on You —

until all the windows
of the Kingdom shine
and we can all be very sure
You wanted every one.

       Bless us, Lord of Heaven,
       Bless us, Mary's child,
       and keep our courage high with You
       through steep and storm and wild.

We are not Poor, not Rich

Rita tends to see
the earth vanish she stands on
just as she lifts each foot
(you keep on going on)
but seeing Vivian with wheels
    and on a road prepared
presumes her terms translate
into undoggedness innate,
i.e., going by vehicle -- not on foot.

Yet Vivian, driving, knows
whirling uncertainties
and simply keeps on, as she goes,
as Rita does.

And I can barely snatch
my foot free when the soppy sand
goes slack
and fills in my old track.
Yet looking up from this Despond, I note
a pilgrim firm of foot
and think he's on a better road
            — and think then wrong.

Speeding by the unmoving is
for each alike a known
blessedness not our own.
And each, in that, goes on.

Transients

The affluent city shaves the turfs
(laid one sun-streamy March morning)
by tractor-mower, tenders them chlorinated
and fluoridated rain from
sunken spigots through a wib-wab spiderly
sprinkler.
              And in July a high-rise
enterprising developer, to
excavate, up roots
the lawnstuff, uncouples the subsurface
aqueduction system.   The city
waits alert even with all that
dirt blowing in its August eyes:
            ready to spread another quilt, in squares
            somewhat rough and ravelled, from
            truckload stores of good fat cakes of grass.

The city ("it" I called us),
fluent, unruffled by February sop-root
or Labour Day cloth-&-sticks,
lights up at night.
It lays and trims and turfs up and
replenishes and hardens in vacant lots and
parking lots.   We are forever
doing, done-to.

           The grass grows
           strongly, it has twitchgrass in
           it too, ready even
           to shag the tracks and blocks
           if we fall
           silent or
           simply let be.

To a Pioneer in Canadian Studies; And to all in such Pedantry

"Give me the camp-out times"
said the prospector.
"Then when the floor gets dirty you move on
upstream and build your fire
on the clean rock, and make you up a
springy cedar mattress...."

Sweeping on those old floors
he left (after the blizzards and the buzzards) for
traces of transient life
is work.   In your steel vertical files
old sweet woodsmoke aromas and
springwater bubbling out and beargrease
so cherished, vanish.
Blinkered graduate students peer
with you in the green light
through memory mesh.   You are
breathing — o, carefully, untouching
Canada in the cocoon there, as it were.

Serving and preserving, you together
may yet perpetuate
the thankless pioneer,
and when the campsite is a clutter
move on, to the clean ancient sunwhite rock.

Speleologist

The seller of irrelevant sweets,
souvenirs, and tickets to the caves,
in a board booth
in an upland pasture
on a September Sunday (gold
and grey above-ground;
bat-coloured, earthworm coloured,
oozing, below)

           is not a seller in a booth
           really, not a
           scientist, excavator, engineer,
           adventurer, enterpreneur
               amongst tourists, really —

he is the naked hiding poignant face
of an earthwork, himself, of centuries,
inevitably the one to
spy out a place of rushing
underground rivers and to break
through, wade in, raft blindly down,
wriggle up soapy chimneys niched for nothingness
   in tinkling total dark,
knowing all rock-webbed vaults,
               arches, hollownesses,
as if beyond the reach of light.

           For he is there,
           himself, though in his odd board booth
           in the September sunlight dozing over
tickets, or (hazily) pop-frigidaire,
cash register.

A Blurt on Gray

I hear far off the unseen:
in 1940, war
from Canada became
all ear-shell and eye-glaze.

Now, in the small-wars-decades
under the newly rainwashed roof
lying by open windows
I hear far off the unseen
wedding party's horns
within a Saturday of garish and drift.

I remember a 1940 wedding
not far from Montreal, in June:
all alone, in
a deep-green hedged field, sunken
in the steeped lingering light;
the rocky outcrop and bunched cedars
breathed gray and stillness.   And
there, well I knew
how this place framed the tank and flare,
the bloody set-up, booming oceans away.

To hear far off the unseen
can make a here of there
without absolving one from having been
summoned to home or being
enlisted here at home.

Absolute

Right here on earth
I've known One Person who would
see me in the worst there is

at the core of it — see me
      e.g. the mocker making a frail rabbi
      hop on the Warsaw pavement yes at the worst
                            would see me
      lazing and lording it over him or e.g. nobody
                        making me do it
    willing to hop on the pavement
    fearful nobody really
       making me
  or e.g. would see me
    turning away from both   in
       order
    to be beautifully alone —

one Person who would
nevertheless care
enough not to be past
tears   *lacrimae*   would never be past minding that
      I'd broken the good
        lost the best
        gone past the most I'd ever ask or hope for

It transfixes,   finding
Someone who means risking
tireless loss
in a real world   e.g.

     along the lake road   with evening pale already
       and nowhere to turn off:
        right here on earth.

Embattled Deliverance

These thinning woods and dry
meadows and scored bluff,
guerrilla nor refugee
find mutually enough

to thatch, let alone nourish
their elusive corps:
eyes flicker at twig-touch and
too near at night earth seeps.

Thump and faint dab of fire
from the great powerfuls
is ungermane; a far
din defines silences.

Come as it may, the clinch
finds ones, gashed (shin or forearm)
but longing for the once
winning, the lustral corpus.

Christ, bright of hope, be
there, calm with your tapers,
in ceremonial care of
our tremulous ardour's.

Poem on the Astronauts in Apollo XIII's Near-Disaster,
written April 17-18, 1970, for the newspaper

Friday a.m.

Intrepid the three are who
out past the blue
float
powerless almost, without
washed air, become almost
morsels of earth-lost dust.

The crippled spacecraft will
bring them back home, if all
earth-generated beams
of intelligent response
to all that may occur still
keep them criss-crossed, can forestall
disasters, one by one.

Friday p.m.

They are safe down,
the representative men
in a representative planet, not left alone
when the air and power were very nearly gone.

Saturday

We in our millions cruise along
in the encapsuling blue
not sure why we belong
on earthship's crew,
all at some instant scared
to find ourselves aboard
and not sure what to do
for safety or for rescue.

A Man could launch the lot
and did so.
John the beloved ("all things were made
by Him") says this is true.
And our hearts and stomachs for this are
thought

spaceworthy, valued at
more than the ride, too.
What of the where and why?
Let easy analogues die
on our lips — we float, not "fly",
keeping check on the fading air and power
supply.

Air-burn, the ocean, divers, nets and decks,
    quarantine, doctors, complex
        debriefing days
are not the NOW that grips all our energies
as knowing, both the dark possibilities
and the bright, grows.

Kahoutek

The comet
among us sun and planets
I saw with naked eye, i.e.
nothing between my ice-
    keening
    tear-washed
    seeing
    from earth-mound (here) to
ocean-deep navy-blue out-there (there).

        In the traffic-flow
        a frozen lump
        from a jolting fender
        spins meteor-black
        towards the midwinter bus-stop where I stand
        under the tall curved night.

Veering weird-brightness
from somewhere else:
we solar-system people flinch
        as at a doom-sign,
and find you cryptic
    from far unlanguaged precincts
        soundlessly hollowing past us.

My tongue, palate, lips, teeth, life's breath,
pronounce "comet", call off
as told
how many million miles away
I with the naked eye still-standing see
you, it —
of quite another orbit.

Seed of snow
    on cement, ditch-rut, rink-steel, salted where
    grass straws thinly scrape against lowering
    daydark in the rise of the earth-crust there
    (and beyond, the scavenging birds
            flitter and skim)
is particle
    unto earth's thirsting,
    spring rain,
    well-spring.
    Roadwork, earthwork, pits in hillsides,
    desolation, abandoned roadside shacks
    and dwelt in,
    unkilned pottery broken and strawed about,
    minibrick people-palaces,
    coming and going always
    by day all lump and ache,
is sown tonight with the beauty
    of light and moving lights, light travelling, light
    shining from beyond farthestness.

Until Christmas

When the maiden consented
the angel departed.

All glory was muted
once the shepherds heeded.

The all He created
hangs on this infant —

helplessly human,
son, God only,

light's focus and source
now sped towards the Cross;

yes, and now in glory
quickening love and longing,

till the angel of His presence
becomes our Christmas incense.

Slow Advent

In silver candy seeds
worked into shortbreads,
a manger and
pentangle star
      — oh, how to utter?
The all-enabling Infant "lulled"
in romance verses,
and plaster, painted, amidst stagehands'
hay and incense
      — oh, how to express
         even the animal *richesse?*
Stitched in wool
on kindergarten paper and
in electrical street-dangles, aglow,
the emblems
      — oh, I too desecrate
      the holy hush
        to trumpet:

Joy in the newborn, so
far, His
coming, so
small to all my anticipating sense of
majesty, yet

indomitably coming:
the flint-set-faced
ready-for-gallows One,
on, on, into glory, and His
place of my being to be
His   as will every
place
be.

Christmas: Becoming

The Breath — flower-gentle, in,
is Word of power, out:
creating that invisible City, and
mountain,   forest,   sea,
tundra,   ore-vein,   light.
         I knew it was forever, for I was young.

The world one day
cracked.
Faces all went gray,
cords, slack.
         I lived towards the mortal Friday for-
                        ever till caught
                            in this.

A stranger flesh
of only son of man
torn and entombed, but raised
timeless, then
         — the eyes turning to look up blur before him —

is still the Christmas presence,
flower-frail, approachable:
the timeless Father does not leave
us broken, in our trouble.

         Even citied, at sea, shop-bound,
           the *here* is veined
             in light.

Midsummer Christmas

Blind under dazzle, aggrieved, held together by
knacks and knuckles, our
warfulness waits.

Don't come here, Jesus!
No.
What You must know here
who can, unless to the obliteration of
the flower-light of Beyond,
                              the far, still hope?

And yet,
oh light us epiphany in humid July!

Behind the open casements and French windows,
in the pantry
in the parlour and window-seat, in
cupboards, velvet
cutlery cases, everywhere
is preparation for
festivity.

He comes.
He left His name, letting it be
given to parents, shepherds, temple habitués,
the village, friends, courts,
executioners, the
Ghost-jubilant; and now
to July's children it is given.

Waking and Sleeping: Christmas

A frontier woman felt
awe, the same awe, she said,
at childbirth and a dying bed.
Yes, said the doctor,
tremblings that reach your heart.

       Too few
       have to know these enough
       and specialties and techniques grow
       that ward exposure off.

Isaac went confidently up the slopes
in Abraham's shadow, unaware
until the sacrificer's knife flashed up:
then the branched ram was there.

       We carol as our earth
       swings some to outer nightward
       and sunfloods the Antipodes (sing forth
       we both, in seasons sundered!)

The newborn in his mortal fairness
moved those shepherds, and the Asian savants,
from other, usual, bent and stress,
to helpless, awestruck jubilance.

But hard on the manger vigil
came Herod's massacre — like
the Pharoah's once — and Rachel's
heart then broke.

       Outside, the hills, sea, sky
       wait — mild.   And welling
       from past the horizoning why
       a new light flows, is filling:

       coming far down, away
       from the enduring Father,

the Child, alone, sets out upon His way
to the cursed tree, His altar.

People tremble and yearn;
our dark hearts thud
in case that light will burn
and wake the dead.

Then

The leopard and the kid
  are smoothness (fierce)
  and softness (gentle)
      and will lie down together.
Then, storm and salt and largeness, known, in time,
      will be within the wholely pure,
              the unimaginable!

   Then, the fair blue
   will not be star-extinguishing;
   and one cascading meadowlark
   an all-where will not deafen;
   acute, prefiguring moments
   of our leaf-flickered day
       will lose none of their poignancy
           when they are caught up, Then, in the
           all-things-upgathering bliss.

   Here, then, prophetically,
   in the strange peace of the outcast
   on manger hay
   lies a real baby:

               all-cherishing, the unsourced,
               the never fully celebrated
               well-spring of That Day.

Creative Hour

The universe our colouring-book:
    "Child, fill it in"? —
or a waxy page to scribbling shade in, and make
streaky pictures come plain?

The outlines vanish.
The tentative image fails.
Chalks smear, all the paint spills,
creation crumples and curls.

I'm down to bone and awe.
Where is this then —
no clock, no lunch, no law?

What is learned, I unlearn:
and hunt out an art school
that may require a model;
or contribute a membership as an art patron;
or, anticipating the generations unborn,
set about knowing what the subjects mean
and how artists have done.

The evasive "maker"-metaphor,
thank God, under the power
of our real common lot
leads stumbling back to what it promised to evade.

There is no one reviewed, no viewer,
no one of us not creature;
we're apparently at work.   But nothing is made
except by the only unpretentious, Jesus Christ, the Lord.

Research

Do your children have nightmares?
said the doctor to the parents.
                    (The wallowing monster;
                    the hairless purple face;
                    an elbow out from under the bed;
                    and that turned-to-marble chase....)
"Yes.
Signals of sickness,
or punishments they dread,
or something they have seen that preys
on their minds till they understand."

The doctor asked the children
whether they thought
adults had nightmares.
                    (When that chalk-blunt thing walks
                    across the green evening — with a
                              broken elbow-hinge,
                      not gumless, not
                    darker in breath among the airs that
                                    stir
                    along the floor of evening, but
                      nudging —
                    in sick distaste, people
                    swing doors against the sky
                    and sealed in lit boxes ask
                    no questions. The doorknob doesn't
                                  twist again.
                    Picturing that bland pace,
                      the forearm jolting loose,
                      makes night's palate dry.
                    The caves along that cliff are
                    left to the gannets.)
"No. They go about
bright rooms till late.

They know where
they are."

All sleep.   And discover
they're child and forebear,
both, together.

From Age to Age: Found Poem

The steady streetcar windows
pass the window squares
of the department stores:
this is Toronto, queen
city, Queen Street.   Next come
the flashing, flowering, high-crest-
low-fall-and-level-shine
City Hall fountains

and in the back of the streetcar here
rises the voice of the morning
                    WAH-TEE!
as in the morning day
when Adam names the animals.

Then the light sharpens;
suddenly shaman di-
dactic, he cries:
                    *LOOK*IT the *Wa*tee mommy!

Stop succeeds stop.
The day flows over him.
He communes here, absorbed, confiding,
at one:
            ("oo ... oh ... watee!")

Is it all past?
He murmurs still ("hmm ... hm") grounding
elation and surprise.
Storm clouds, dove-grey,
eclipse the blue and gold.

West farther still
every windowed car will be
threaded through
the far lake light and the reflective low
waters of Grenadier Pond.

Wonder: a Street-car Sketch

Judgment as well as mercy:
   that these could fuse
      is staggering.

   A little girl at an open window
   blown wildly, safe beside
   her mother (on the aisle) is flooded by
   colour, motion, glass-shine, sidewalk marvels
   blowing and jewelling in.
   All alerted, she turns
   unable to bear alone the pour of wonder.

   The strong young mother (is she fighting sleep?)
   steady in the bucking and swaying car
   has one arm up, stiff, palm over the eyes.

   The little girl cries "peek aboo!" and
   yanks at the awkward elbow
   baring (oh, she is weeping)
   the wet and swollen flesh
   eyeless as a fair and quiet moon
   suddenly at crash-down range.

   Briefly they are together.
   Then the hand closes down.
   But the little one's face does not crumple
   or burrow; with a flickering smile
   she snuggles confidently
   back, absorbed with the now
   limited wonder still.

The stricken moment,
our Elder Brother's, glimpsed,
is inexplicably
left His for now:
             we marvel
             far off, however near, in
             limited wonder still.

SKETCH: *Child in Subway*

A whirr of dry air
    cement crumbs   cinders   newspaper scraps
        grits the eyelashes from
            the people-bobbled stairs down to the subway.

A child, stumbling at the steepness
and the hurrying   hurrying,
hangs on, then boldly tread-skims
the steps on his parents' arm-ends,
heading eagerly towards
brake-scream, train-rush,
door-clatter, plastic glare and tunnel-plunge,

        wherever his day's lifetime may
        go in its faithful unpredictability.

Bereaved

The children's voices
      all red and blue and green in the
      queer April dimness —
      just as in Ur, at dusk, under the walls —

      are a barbarous tongue,   lost on
      that unmirroring, immured,
      that thumping thing,
             the heavy adult heart.

The children's voices are
the immemorial chorus.